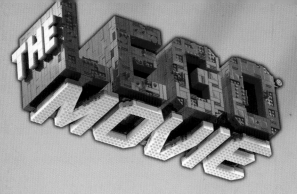

THE OFFICIAL
MOVIE
HANDBOOK

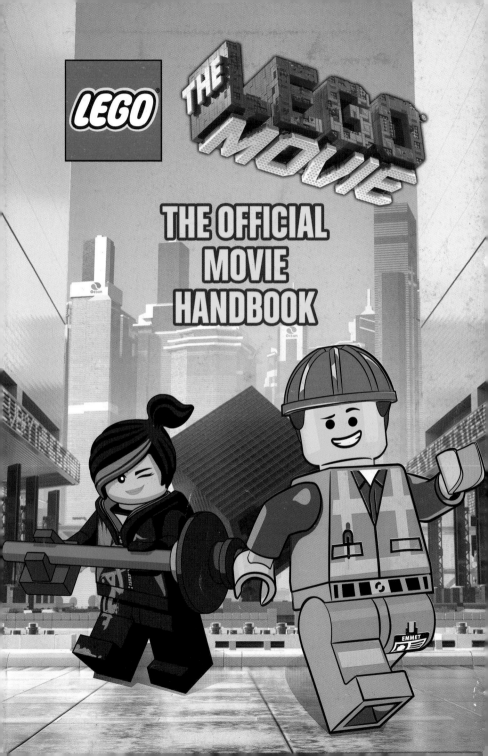

LEGO®

THE LEGO MOVIE

THE OFFICIAL MOVIE HANDBOOK

Ladybird

Published by Ladybird Books Ltd 2014
A Penguin Company
Penguin Books Ltd, 80 Strand, London, WC2R 0RL, UK
Penguin Books Australia Ltd, 707 Collins Street, Melbourne,
Victoria 3008, Australia (a division of Pearson Australia
Group Pty Ltd)

www.ladybird.com

Written by Ace Landers
Based on the screenplay by Phil Lord and Christopher Miller
Based on the story by Dan Hageman and Kevin Hageman and
Phil Lord & Christopher Milller
Designed by Two Red Shoes Design Inc.
Cover and additional illustrations by Kenny Kiernan

 Produced by AMEET Sp. z o.o.
under license from the LEGO Group.

AMEET Sp. z o.o.,
Nowe Sady 6, 94-102 Łódź – Poland
ameet@ameet.pl
www.ameet.pl

Penguin Books Ltd, 80 Strand, London, WC2R 0RL, UK
Please keep the Penguin Books Ltd address for future reference.

www.LEGO.com

ISBN: 9780723293361

002

Printed in Poland

Item name: THE OFFICIAL MOVIE HANDBOOK
Series: LMH
Item number: LMH-101
Batch: 02/GB

CONTENTS

Welcome to Bricksburg 6

Emmet 8

Wyldstyle 14

Vitruvius 18

Lord Business 20

President Business 22

Bad Cop 26

Where Are My Pants? 28

Batman™ 34

UniKitty 36

Benny 38

Metal Beard 40

Bricksburg 44

Octan Corporation 46

The Construction Site 48

The Wild West 50

Cloud Cuckoo Land 52

The LEGO® Movie Sneak Peek 56

Welcome to
BRICKSBURG

Hello, citizen! Thanks for joining us in the wonderful world of Bricksburg!

Every day in our beautiful city is a great day, because all of our citizens are always super happy. Emmet is one of Bricksburg's favourite citizens and he's here to tell you why everything in the city is so awesome.

HEY, THAT'S ME! COME ON, LET'S GO!

EMMET

Emmet

HI! I'M EMMET AND I'M A HAPPY CONSTRUCTION WORKER LIVING IN THE BEST CITY EVER - BRICKSBURG! WOW, I'VE JUST REALISED I'M IN A BOOK ABOUT MY FAVOURITE PLACE...THAT'S SO COOL!

SPEAKING OF BOOKS, HAVE YOU READ **HOW TO FIT IN, HAVE EVERYONE LIKE YOU, AND ALWAYS BE HAPPY**? I ALWAYS KEEP A COPY TO HAND. IT GIVES YOU STEP-BY-STEP INSTRUCTIONS ON HOW TO HAVE AN AWESOME DAY! HERE, LET ME SHOW YOU!

EMMET

HOW TO:

FIT IN

0-99
6981
STEP-BY-STEP INSTRUCTIONS!

HAVE EVERYONE LIKE YOU

AND ALWAYS BE HAPPY

 HERE ARE MY FIVE FAVOURITE STEPS TO START THE DAY.

STEP 1: Breathe.

It's easier than it looks. I can almost do it without thinking.

STEP 2: Exercise.

I am so pumped up!

STEP 3: Shower and get dressed.

But not at the same time. I tried that once. It didn't go too well.

STEP 4: Enjoy popular songs, like *Everything is Awesome* and watch cool television shows, like *Where Are My Pants?*

where are my pants?

Ha ha — where ARE his pants?

STEP 5: And always obey President Business's instructions or you'll be put to sleep.

This guy is so cool! I always want to hear more of what he has to say.

SEE, IT'S SO EASY TO . . . WAIT, DID THAT LAST RULE SAY "PUT TO SLEEP"?!

EVERYTHING IS AWESOME

OH, MAN, I LOVE THAT SONG! WHAT WAS I SAYING? EH, I DON'T CARE.

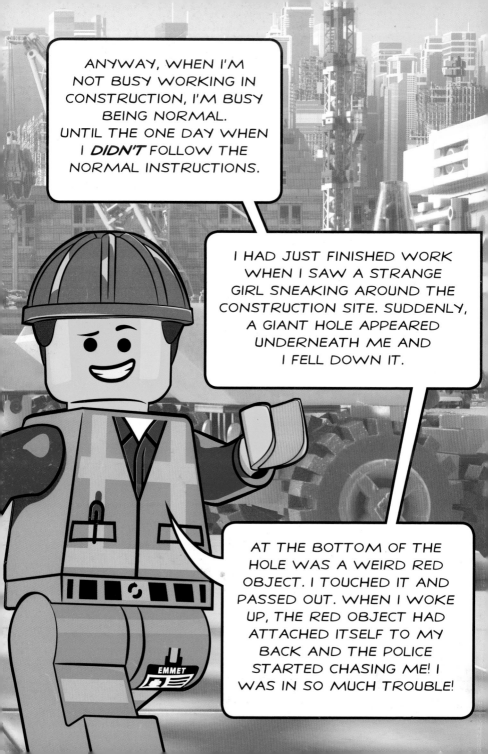

Me following the instructions. See how happy I was?

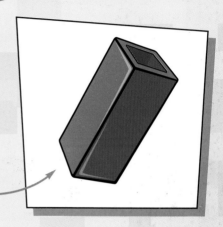

Then THIS weird thing got stuck on my back.

And now the police are chasing me. This is NOT cool!

I THOUGHT I WAS A GONER WHEN, OUT OF NOWHERE, THAT STRANGE GIRL SHOWED UP AGAIN AND SAVED ME.

THAT DOESN'T MATTER NOW. ALL THAT MATTERS IS THE THING ATTACHED TO YOUR BACK. IT'S THE **PIECE OF RESISTANCE** AND THE ONLY THING THAT CAN STOP PRESIDENT BUSINESS'S PLAN TO GLUE THE WORLD TOGETHER.

THERE'S A PROPHECY THAT SAYS ONE PERSON, **THE SPECIAL**, WILL FIND THE PIECE OF RESISTANCE AND SAVE THE WORLD. IT ALSO SAYS THAT HE OR SHE WILL BE THE MOST IMPORTANT AND EXTRAORDINARY PERSON IN THE UNIVERSE! THAT MUST BE YOU, RIGHT?

UMMM... YEAH. RIGHT ... THAT MUST BE ME! ALL THOSE **AWESOME** THINGS THAT YOU JUST SAID!

I'M PART OF AN UNDERGROUND REBELLION CALLED THE **MASTER BUILDERS**. WE HAVE VOWED TO STOP LORD BUSINESS, OR PRESIDENT BUSINESS AS YOU KNOW HIM.

EVERY MASTER BUILDER CAN **"QUICKBUILD"** NEW OBJECTS OUT OF ORDINARY PIECES LYING AROUND WITHOUT FOLLOWING THE INSTRUCTIONS. JUST WATCH.

NEED A MOTORCYCLE? BAM!

NEED A MOTOR-PLA... BAM!

WHOA, YOU SOUND COOL!

THANKS. NOW COME ON. WE NEED TO GO SEE VITRUVIUS! HE'LL TELL US HOW TO USE THE PIECE OF RESISTANCE TO SAVE THE WORLD.

THE PROPHECY

One day a talented lass or fellow,
a Special One with face of yellow,
will make the Piece of Resistance found
from its hiding refuge underground.
And with a noble army at the helm,
this Master Builder will thwart
the Kragle and save the realm,
and be the greatest, most interesting,
most important person of all times.
All this is true because it rhymes.

LORD BUSINESS

DON'T LET LORD BUSINESS'S FRIENDLY DISGUISE AS "PRESIDENT BUSINESS" FOOL YOU. HE IS ONE OF THE MOST DEVIOUS PEOPLE YOU'LL EVER MEET.

FOR YEARS I KEPT THE KRAGLE HIDDEN. BUT HE CAME AFTER IT, AND I WAS BLINDED IN THE BATTLE.

THAT'S RIGHT. I'M MISTER BIG BOY PANTS AND THE KRAGLE IS MINE, OLD MAN. **ALL MINE! MWAHAHAHAHA!**

THE KRAGLE IS A WEAPON THAT SHOOTS LASER BEAMS OF GLUE. LORD BUSINESS WANTS EVERYTHING TO STAY HIS WAY, SO HE'S GOING TO GLUE OUR WHOLE WORLD TOGETHER!

BUT IF THE KRAGLE IS CAPPED BY THE PIECE OF RESISTANCE, IT WILL LOSE ITS POWER. EMMET, YOU AND AN ARMY OF MASTER BUILDERS MUST STORM LORD BUSINESS'S TOWER TO STOP HIM AND SAVE THE WORLD.

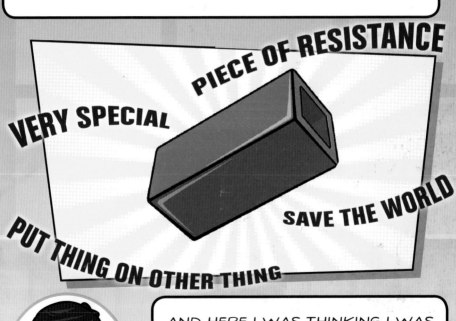

PIECE OF RESISTANCE

VERY SPECIAL

SAVE THE WORLD

PUT THING ON OTHER THING

AND HERE I WAS THINKING I WAS JUST NARRATING A BOOK ABOUT BRICKSBURG. THIS IS TURNING INTO A VERY WEIRD DAY...

PRESIDENT BUSINESS

HEY, PAL! I'M PRESIDENT BUSINESS, THE OWNER, FOUNDER AND PRESIDENT OF THE OCTAN CORPORATION . . . **AND THE WORLD.**

WE HERE AT OCTAN KNOW HOW HARD IT IS TO FIT IN AND HAVE EVERYONE LIKE YOU. SO, WE WANT TO SHARE OUR YEARS OF EXPERIENCE WITH YOU. IT'S A SIMPLE RECIPE FOR SUCCESS. JUST FOLLOW THE INSTRUCTIONS. **MY INSTRUCTIONS.**

WHAT CAN I SAY? OVERLORDING IS MY BUSINESS AND BUSINESS IS GOOD. BUT SINCE THE WORLD IS COMING TO AN EN — I MEAN, SINCE IT'S ALMOST TACO TUESDAY, I SUPPOSE I CAN SHARE SOME OF MY TRADE SECRETS WITH YOU.

How to Conquer the Universe While Making Everyone Love You!

Step 1:
Take time to meditate before every busy day of conquering.

Step 2:
Amass a great deal of power by any means necessary. Like offering free tacos!

Step 3:
Impose rules. Lots and lots of rules.

BECAUSE I SAID SO!

I WANT YOU... TO FOLLOW THE INSTRUCTIONS!

BAD COP

OF COURSE, I CAN'T DO ALL THIS OVERLORDING ON MY OWN. MEET BAD COP, MY HENCHIEST OF HENCHMEN. WE'VE DONE SOME GREAT WORK TOGETHER OVER THE YEARS.

POLICED TO MEET YOU. ANYONE WHO GETS IN MY WAY IS GOING DOWN. LITERALLY AND METAPHORICALLY.

BATMAN

FIRST, WE HAVE BATMAN. HE'S AN INCREDIBLE, SUPER-DREAMY SUPERHERO. OH, AND HE'S ALSO MY BOYFRIEND.

I'M BATMAN.

BATMAN'S YOUR **BOYFRIEND?!**

I'LL TAKE IT FROM HERE, BABE. YEAH, THAT'S RIGHT, I'M THE CAPED CRUSADER AND I'VE BROUGHT PLENTY OF TOYS TO THE PARTY. THE BATWING, THE BATMOBILE, BATARANGS – ALL IN BLACK. AND SOME IN VERY, VERY DARK GREY. LORD BUSINESS IS GOING DOWN. JUST DON'T GET IN MY WAY. BATMAN WORKS ALONE.

I'M A MASKED MAN OF JUSTICE. I'VE GOT A FANTASTIC BELT AND A DEEP SUPERHERO VOICE. I'M BATMAN.

YOU ALREADY SAID THAT!

SIGH. HE'S SOOO DARK AND BROODING.

unikitty

THEN WE HAVE UNIKITTY, THE MOST BUBBLY UNICORN-KITTY HYBRID YOU'LL EVER MEET. SHE LIVES IN CLOUD CUCKOO LAND – A CRAZY, COLOURFUL WONDERLAND WITH NO RULES WHATSOEVER.

ANY IDEA IS A GOOD IDEA, EXCEPT THE NOT HAPPY ONES!

Hiiiii!

Hiiiii! I am Princess UniKitty, and I welcome you all to my mega-dreamy dream journal for my **bestest friends** in the whole wide world!

I know just the way to stop Lord Business from spreading unhappy thoughts. He just needs to see how much fun the happy thoughts are! For example:

What are your fave colours? Mine change every day, but right now I totally **love** mountain cherry, extreme watermelon and sour apple.

And always remember, any idea is a good idea. Except the **not happy** ones.

BUT SOMETIMES, WHEN I THINK ABOUT LORD BUSINESS'S PLAN, I START TO FEEL SOMETHING INSIDE...LIKE THE OPPOSITE OF HAPPINESS. I MUST...STAY POSITIVE...BUBBLE GUM... BUTTERFLIES...GRRRR!

BENNY

REMEMBER THE FIRST ASTRONAUTS WHO WENT INTO SPACE? WELL, THIS IS BENNY, A CLASSIC SPACEMAN FROM 1980-SOMETHING. HE'S A LITTLE OBSESSED WITH SPACESHIPS.

IF WE'RE GOING TO STOP LORD BUSINESS, WE NEED TO GET TO HIS TOWER. AND THAT MEANS WE NEED A . . . SPACESHIP!

METAL BEARD

THIS SWISS ARMY PIRATE IS METAL BEARD. SURE, HE'S CRAGGY, BUT WOULDN'T YOU BE IF YOU LOST YOUR BODY IN A BATTLE WITH LORD BUSINESS?

CAPTAIN'S LOG

ARRGH. WE TRIED TO STORM LORD BUSINESS'S TOWER TODAY. WE USED EVERY PLAN WE COULD THINK OF. THE RESULT WAS A MASSACRE TOO TERRIBLE TO SPEAK OF. BUT HERE GOES...

GUARDED BY A ROBOT ARMY, LASERS, SHARKS, OVERBEARING ASSISTANTS AND STRANGE, DANGEROUS RELICS THAT ENTRAP, SNAP AND ZAP.

I LOST ME CREW. I LOST ME BODY. ME ORGANS WERE STREWN HITHER AND YON. I HAD TO STOW ME ORGANS IN A SEA CHEST AND REPLACE EVERY PART OF ME ONCE-STRAPPING PIRATE BODY WITH THIS USELESS HUNK OF GARBAGE YE SEE BEFORE YE. ARRR, IT MAKES ME FURIOUS!

HMM, I'M KIND OF ATTACHED TO MY BODY, SO I PROBABLY WOULDN'T LIKE LOSING IT. THOUGH IT MIGHT BE COOL TO HAVE A SHARK FOR AN ARM.

HELLO, FRIENDS. VITRUVIUS HERE. BEFORE YOU CAN JOIN EMMET AND WYLDSTYLE ON THEIR ADVENTURE, YOU SHOULD KNOW ABOUT THE DIFFERENT REALMS IN THE UNIVERSE.

BRICKSBURG IS BUT ONE SMALL CORNER OF THIS DOMAIN. THERE ARE MANY DIFFERENT WORLDS TO EXPLORE. LORD BUSINESS BUILT WALLS BETWEEN THEM, BUT WE MASTER BUILDERS CREATED SECRET TUNNELS ALLOWING US TO PASS BETWEEN THE REALMS.

FOLLOW ME AND I WILL BE YOUR GUIDE. UMM, BUT FIRST, WILL YOU HELP ME FIND THE NEXT PAGE?

THE BUSTLING METROPOLIS OF BRICKSBURG IS A CITY BUILT ON INSTRUCTIONS. EVERYONE PARKS BETWEEN THE LINES, DROPS OFF THEIR DRY CLEANING BEFORE NOON AND NEVER FORGETS TO SMILE. BUT THERE IS A SECRET BENEATH BRICKSBURG'S SEEMING "PERFECTION."

OCTAN CORPORATION

THE CONSTRUCTION SITE

THIS IS THE CONSTRUCTION SITE WHERE EMMET WORKS. AFTER A LONG DAY, THE CREW MEMBERS ALWAYS GO OUT TO EAT CHICKEN WINGS AND GET *CRAZY*. NORMALLY, EMMET WOULD JOIN THEM. BUT ON THAT ONE, FATEFUL AFTERNOON, THIS IS THE PLACE EMMET FOUND THE PIECE OF RESISTANCE AND HIS LIFE CHANGED FOREVER.

I'M NOT GONNA LIE. THAT WAS A VERY WEIRD DAY.

THE WILD WEST

THERE'S PLENTY OF TROUBLE BREWING IN THIS ONE-HORSE TOWN. LORD BUSINESS'S ROBOTS ARE ALWAYS ON WATCH. THE ROBOTS INCLUDE DEPUTRON, CALAMITY DRONE, WILEY FUSEBOT AND SHERIFF NOT-A-ROBOT. YET, I CALL THE WILD WEST HOME. WHAT BETTER PLACE IS THERE TO HIDE OUT IF YOU'RE A BLIND WIZARD WHO CAN PLAY A MEAN PIANO TUNE?

THAT MAKES, LIKE, ZERO SENSE.

CLOUD CUCKOO LAND

THIS WACKY INSIDE-OUT, UPSIDE-DOWN REALM THRIVES ON PURE CREATIVITY. THIS IS WHERE WE MASTER BUILDERS GATHER TO FORM OUR PLAN TO DEFEAT LORD BUSINESS. HOWEVER, THE PROPHECY DIDN'T PLAY OUT EXACTLY AS WE THOUGHT.

And now, a sneak peek at the new LEGO Movie!

One average morning in the city of Bricksburg, Emmet, the most regular guy in the world, woke up the same way he did every day. He followed his book of instructions on how to fit in and ran through his normal morning routine.

He greeted the day, smiled, did jumping jacks, ate breakfast and watched popular television shows on TV. Then he went to work.

A POPULAR BAND

But what Emmet didn't know was that everything was about to change. Today would be the beginning of the most un-normal adventure of his entire life.

Emmet worked for a construction company that demolished every weird, creative building in Bricksburg. They replaced them with identical skyscrapers that always followed the instructions. No one knew why the buildings had to look the same. But those were the rules. And everyone knew that the best way to be happy was to follow the rules.

After work, Emmet had planned to join his coworkers for a night of delicious chicken wings. But just as he was leaving, a gust of wind blew his instructions out of his hand. He had just chased them down when, suddenly, Emmet saw a mysterious girl, who wasn't supposed to be on the building site, digging through a pile of rubble.

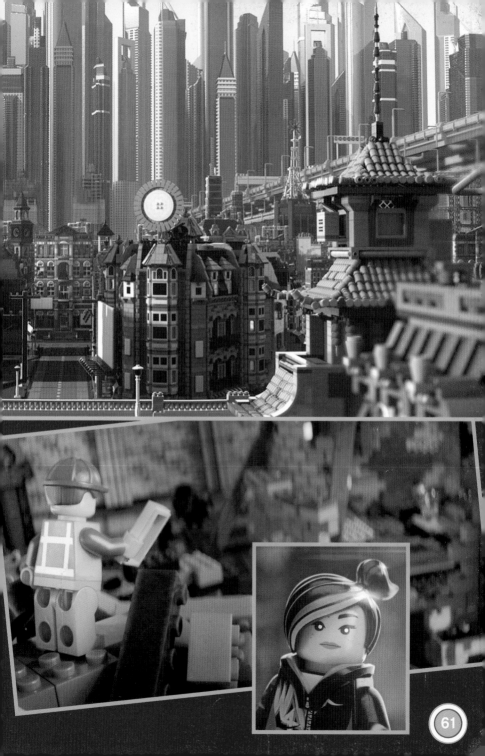

When Emmet tried to follow the girl, the rubble below him cracked open and he fell down into a huge hole! He yelled as he tumbled through the air, until he finally landed at the very bottom.

When Emmet looked up, he couldn't understand what he was seeing. Sitting in front of him was a strange-looking object glowing bright red. It was like nothing he had ever seen in Bricksburg. It was like nothing he had ever seen in his life. Emmet couldn't help himself. He touched it.

Instantly, a glaring white light flashed and Emmet passed out.

When he woke up, Emmet had no idea where he was. He was strapped to a chair in a strange place and a very angry police officer was glaring at him from across a table. This was Bad Cop – the meanest, most ruthless officer in all of Bricksburg.

And he had one very important question for Emmet:
"How did you find the Piece of Resistance?!"

*Find out the rest of Emmet's incredible story
in the new LEGO Movie!*

THE LEGO MOVIE